It Starts with Self-Love:
The Secret to Improve Your Confidence, Build Better Relationships, and Live a Happier Life

Jennifer N. Smith

Copyright and Disclaimer

CONTENTS

Introduction

Is life unfair? Do you think that you deserve a better life, but feel trapped in the situation you're in? If your answer is "yes" to these questions, then **today is the day that you take charge and make a change in your life.**

First, I want you to realize that the only reason that's holding you back from having a better life is you! That's right, Y-O-U. This might be hard for you to understand right now, but as you read through this book, **you will understand that you play a big role in how your life is turning out.**

The reason why most of us trapped in a crappy life is because we allow ourselves to be trapped. The only reason why you can't move forward is because you don't know how to let go of the past. The doubts you're having and the fear of failing again are the only reasons why opportunities seem scarce for you.

Now the question is, how do you turn things around? How do you find the key to a better life? Well, the answer to that is simple, and that's SELF-LOVE.

By reading the chapters of this book you will understand what self-love is all about and why it will help you become a better person and have a great life. You will also discover the causes of lack of self-love and how it effects your life. And how you can forgive and let go of your past mistakes, how you can trust yourself again and take charge of your life, how you can embrace your uniqueness and use your strengths to build a better life.

I want you to realize that the only reason that's holding you back from having a better life is you! That's right, Y-O-U.

This might be hard for you to understand right now, but as you read through this book, you will understand that you play a big role in how your life is turning out.

You are now at the beginning of your journey to having a better life. The road isn't easy and short, but with persistence, you will learn to love yourself again and then eventually share this love to others.

I hope you will be able to unveil the secret to improving your confidence, building great relationships, and living a happier life! Enjoy reading!

Chapter 1: All About Self-Love

Why should I love myself? How can my life become happier when I love myself?

Before you can answer those questions, you have to understand what self-love is. Please don't think that loving yourself is narcissism. There's nothing wrong with loving yourself and celebrating your uniqueness. **However, too much self-love where you become too self-fish and too proud of yourself is wrong.**

The self-love I'm talking about means having self-respect, seeing a positive image of yourself, and accepting yourself for who you are. Encyclopedia.com defines self-love as "regard for one's own well-being and happiness."

But if self-love can make life better, why do other people (probably including you) deprive themselves of self-love?

Causes of Lack of Self-Love

I won't blame you why you feel like you can't forgive yourself and so you deprive yourself of love, because there are many things surround you that gives you even more reasons not to practice self-love.

- **Criticisms**

  Maybe you grew up in a household where your parents are too critical of you that no matter what you did or how hard you tried, your efforts weren't enough.

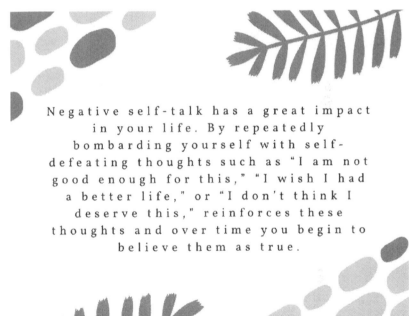

Negative self-talk has a great impact in your life. By repeatedly bombarding yourself with self-defeating thoughts such as "I am not good enough for this," "I wish I had a better life," or "I don't think I deserve this," reinforces these thoughts and over time you begin to believe them as true.

Although probably for your parents, that was their way of showing their love because they pushed you to become better, but these criticisms have affected you in such a great way that when you grew up you started to question every move you make.

- **Bullying**

Maybe you had a rough childhood. Even though your parents showed their all-out support for you, the kids at school teased you and bullied you because you were different. So instead of embracing your individuality you started hating yourself because you were not "normal" and so you ended up forcing yourself to fit in.

- **Habit of Negative Self-talk**

You might not have noticed it, but through the years you have developed the habit of negative-self talk. You may think that this is harmless. How can negative thinking that only happens in your head affect your life, right? But in contrary, negative self-talk has a great impact in your life. By repeatedly bombarding yourself with self-defeating thoughts such as "I am not good enough for this," "I wish I had a better life," or "I don't think I deserve this," reinforces these thoughts and over time you begin to believe them as true. So when an opportunity arises, instead of seizing it, you end up questioning yourself whether you are really up for the opportunity, or whether you really deserve it.

- **Past Failures**

  You probably have experienced too many failures in
  the past that you end up believing that you can't do
  anything right.

- **The Media**

  This may be a surprise for you, but yes, the media—
  the advertisements you see on TV or magazines, or the
  posts you see on social media could make you feel bad
  about yourself. Because it made us believe that having
  a bikini body, a nice car and house, owning the latest
  gadgets and having the means to spend on a luxurious
  vacation .... so on are only the ways to be loved and
  be happy, **but this is not true.**

You might identify at least one of these reasons why you lack
self-love, but whatever the reason, I want you to understand
that you have the key to free yourself from these things. Yes,
you might be a child of too critical parents, you may be a
victim of bullying, you may have experienced one
unfortunate event after the other, you may be friends with
people who have it all, **but you are the only person who
decides whether you let these things affect you or
not.**

The Effects of Lack of Self-Love

Maybe you don't totally agree with me that self-love is the
key to a happier life, but let me give you concrete examples
on how depriving yourself of self-love can have significant
effects in your life.

- **You begin to hate yourself**- Yes, hate is a strong word, but if you don't love yourself, you will loathe yourself with **negative thoughts**— how you are different from the others, how incapable you are, you are good for nothing, etc. The danger of this kind of attitude is that you have the higher tendency to suffer even more serious psychological disorders such as anxiety and depression that could also lead to self-inflicted harm.

- **You won't feel good enough**- If you lack self-love, you will never be contented with your achievements, even if what you've accomplished is already impressive. Since you think of yourself as a failure, you will have the tendency to see even the minuscule mistakes that you made and **fail to see what you have already attained.**

- **You feel worthless**- Even if people around you try their hardest to make you feel special, if you lack self-love, you will still think that you are worthless. You will still feel that you are a lesser being than everybody around you. You will envelope yourself with pity and thoughts that will paralyze you.

- **You become overly sensitive**- You take criticisms personally, even if it is not directed to you. For example, your boss wants a revision on the proposal that your team submitted. Instead of focusing on what your boss wants you to do, you take his criticisms personally. You feel that he/she rejected the proposal because of you, a failure, were part of it. What's the result? Instead of delivering what he wants, you spent most of your time and energy focusing on your mistakes.

- **You will always try to please others**-Because you believe that you are not good enough, you end up trying to please everybody around you so they can respect and accept you. Unfortunately, **people-pleasers don't usually get what they want, but they only end up being used by others.**

- **You let opportunities pass you by**-Because you doubt yourself and your abilities, even if opportunities are already knocking at your door, you will allow them to pass because you think you are not good enough. What's the result? You miss the chances of having a good life or a great career and you become stuck to where you are.

Reasons to Practice Self-Love

Now you know the causes and effects of why you don't love yourself, I hope you begin loving yourself again. But if not, here are more reasons why you should:

- **Because you open yourself to love** - Wonder why you end up in the wrong relationships? Or why you can't find someone who will love you? I don't know about you, but I'd like to believe that one of the major reasons of this is because you lack self-love.

    You see, I'm a strong believer of the law of attraction—a philosophy that likes attract likes. In this case, if you love yourself, then love from other people will easily come to you.

- **Because people will start to accept you** - How can people accept you for who you are if you don't love yourself and accept yourself? When you begin embracing your uniqueness, people will also start accepting you for who you are. There's no need for you to try to fit in, because people will see how special you are, if you let them see it.

If you lack self-love, you will never be contented with your achievements, even if what you've accomplished is already impressive.

Since you think of yourself as a failure, you will have the tendency to see even the minuscule mistakes that you made and fail to see what you have already attained.

- **Because it is good for your health** – When you love and care about yourself, you will ensure that your health is also in top shape. **You have more motivation to go to the gym and workout, watch over your diet, and take the vitamins and supplements you need to maintain a healthy body.**

- **Because it boosts your confidence**-When you start to practice self-love, the improvement of your confidence follows. If before, you didn't have the guts to speak up during a meeting at your office, because you feel that you're insignificant, practicing self-love will give you the drive to share your thoughts because you know that your ideas matter. **You might not know it, but this extra boost of self-confidence might be the key to the job promotion that you're waiting for.**

- **Because it lowers your risk of developing psychological disorders** – According to many studies; people who practice self-love, or have good self-esteem are emotionally stable, which means they have lesser risks of developing psychological disorders such as anxiety, depression, and even eating disorders.

- **Because it makes getting over your mistakes easier** - As long as we live, we will always be vulnerable to making mistakes; even people who you look up to also make mistakes. But what differentiates people that make it on top to those who are stuck at the bottom is how they bounce back up even after these failures. People who practice self-love doesn't allow these failures to hold them back, they instead, **use them as lessons to better themselves.**

- **Because it improves your self-image** - Even if the majority of people think that the only acceptable body is when you have flat, sexy body that could fit tiny dresses, practicing self-love will not make you hate your body even if you don't fall into this stereotype. If you love yourself, **you will learn how to love your body, imperfections included.**

- **Because it builds great relationships** - Do you hate people who are conceited and are just too full of themselves? Do you see how people avoid and repel being with narcissists? That is the same effect that people feel around individuals who lack self-love. That's why, if you want to start building meaningful relationships that lasts, then you have to start loving yourself first. Again, remember the law of attraction, if you practice self-love, you will attract people who also love themselves; these are the types of people who are optimists, happy, and those who will have a good impact in your life.

Here's the hard truth: **no one will love you if you don't love yourself first**. As soon as you start to love yourself again, it is only then that you are allowing good things to happen in your life. Yes, it sounds easier said than done, **but it is possible.** Turn to the next chapter to see how you can begin!

Chapter 2: Letting Go: Allowing Yourself to Heal

Like I said in the previous chapter, there are many reasons why you lack self-love. Your parents may not be as supportive as others, you have had bad experiences in the past, or you have failed many times even if you think you've done your best. Whatever that reason is, the only way that you can begin loving yourself again is through forgiveness. Allowing yourself to heal is the first step of this long journey.

I'm not saying that you _forget_ what people have done to you or what mistakes you've done in the past, what I'm saying here is for you to _forgive_ and then move on.

Yes, forgiveness is hard, especially if a certain person or situation left a deep scar, **but it is the only way that you can set yourself free.** When you begin to forgive, you are allowing yourself to become better. You are letting go of the grudges, remorse, and pain that you held on for so long. When you forgive, you prove to yourself that you are strong.

Yes! You are strong when you forgive because you can overcome the challenges that happened to you and face the new day with a smile.

Forgiveness is also good for your over-all health, studies show that people who know how to forgive significantly show a decreased risk for depression, reduced feelings of anger, and an improved self-confidence. Most importantly, **allowing yourself to let go of the past means you're allowing yourself to live life to the fullest.**

Forgiveness doesn't come in an instant, _it's a process_. So don't force yourself to get over the situation right away, instead, just be open and allow healing to happen. If you think you're ready to let go of the past, you can use the strategies below to help you in your journey towards forgiveness.

- **Remind Yourself: Past is Past**

  This is probably basic, but most people tend to forget that there's nothing they could do to change the past. When you are able to realize this, then accepting what happened to you, even if how hurtful it is, would be easier.

  So what if you made so many mistakes in the past? Unless you're not aware of it, all people commit mistakes. So what if you failed? These mistakes only mean that you can avoid them the second time around.

  Every new day is an opportunity for you to get over these mistakes and create a different future.

- **Pinpoint the Issue**

What's holding you back from forgiving the person that hurt you? Is it pride? Unresolved issues? Do you think you need closure?

When you begin to forgive, you are allowing yourself to become better. You are letting go of the grudges, remorse, and pain that you held on for so long. When you forgive, you prove to yourself that you are strong.

Yes! You are strong when you forgive because you can overcome the challenges that happened to you and face the new day with a smile.

Why do you avoid relationships? Is it because you were cheated on by who you thought was the love of your life? Why do you avoid your friends? Is it because you hate your body, and you don't want them to see it?

Identify which issues are holding you back. List them down if it helps. Doing this will allow you to tackle them and begin the process of healing.

- **Focus on the Lesson Learned**

  Instead of wallowing yourself in self-pity and thinking about how other people hurt you, or how you've been such a disappointment, ***why don't you have a shift in your mindset and focus on what this challenge has taught you?***

  Do you hate your parents because they were too critical of you? Look at yourself now and see what you have achieved to prove to them that you can accomplish something significant. Aren't you supposed to be thankful because they've pushed you to become a person you didn't even imagine to be?

  Do you hate life because you have to endure one challenge after the other? But have you ever thought that these challenges had molded you to become more resilient? Haven't you become much stronger because of these difficulties?

  Keep in mind that everything happens for a reason, even if hurtful events happens to you one after the next, you will be able to appreciate these things if you just change your mindset.

- **Difficulties Does Not Define Your Life**

  Think of the hurtful things that happened to you and the mistakes that others committed against you is only a part of your life; in fact, it's already a part of your past! Meaning, you have the power not to allow these things to take hold of your ***present and future.*** Do not let these things define your life, let go of these things and choose to live a happier life!

- **Release Resentment**

  Holding grudges and resentment to a person that hurt
  you isn't actually doing damage to that person, **but
  instead, it damages you.** You're the only one who's
  affected when you hold ill feelings to a person that
  hurt you. So why would you let him or her affect you?
  Let go of resentment and you will surely find peace.

- **Try to Make Up for It**

  If for years you've hated what you see in the mirror
  because you've become overweight, my question is,
  have you done something to change it? Forgive
  yourself for chugging down pints of ice creams after
  your break-up, you cannot do anything about that.
  But what you can do is try to make up for it. Instead of
  allowing self-pity, why don't you enroll in a gym, jump
  on a diet program and then start losing weight?

  **Again, even if we cannot do anything that
  happened in the past, all of us are given the
  opportunity to change the future in the
  present.**

- **See these Difficulties as a Challenge**

  Did you have a difficult childhood because your peers
  teased you since you were the tall or an odd looking
  girl? Well, you have the choice—either to try your
  hardest to be sexy and fit in the standards of what
  they define as beautiful, or build on your assets and
  become successful with the gift you have.

• **Do a Forgiveness Ritual**

Think of the hurtful things that happened to you and the mistakes that others committed against you is only a part of your life; in fact, it's already a part of your past! Meaning, you have the power not to allow these things to take hold of your present and future.

Do not let these things define your life, let go of these things and choose to live a happier life!

Some people would find it easier to let go if they did something concrete to begin the process of forgiveness. If you think that a weeklong retreat would help you heal, then by all means do it. Write a letter to the person who hurt you and burn it, if you think that it is the only way you can forgive him/her. Face the mirror and talk to yourself, tell yourself "I forgive you" repeatedly until you've finally allowed yourself to heal.

Find out what "ritual" works for you, the most important thing here is that through this activity, you can let go of your hurtful past.

- **Let Others Know How You Feel**

The process of forgiveness will be easier if you have someone you trust to listen to you and offer words of support. Find a person whom you trust most and share with them your feelings. Tell them why you're hurt and why you think that you don't deserve love. Ask for their advice and listen to what they have to say. This thing alone will help you to vent out the ill feelings you have and will surely help in your healing process.

Remember all of us have the free will to choose whether we live in the past, dread on our mistakes, and be miserable for the rest of our lives, or choose to allow ourselves to move on, forgive others and ourselves, and live a happy life. **If I were to ask you, what will you choose? I hope you choose to be happy!**

Chapter 3: Trusting that You Can

For years, maybe you've been living a life where you always doubted yourself. Maybe since you were young, you never had the confidence to showcase your abilities because you feel like you're never good enough. Well, let me ask you, where did that self-doubt bring you?

Were you able to become successful even if you had doubts in yourself? Were you able to reach impossible goals even if you feel like you're not capable of doing things right? I think not.

My guess is that your self-doubt only created bigger fears. Because you didn't believe in yourself, you let a lot of opportunities to pass you by. You surrounded yourself with barricades, avoiding risks that could propel you to a better life; because you chose to be safe.

If you're tired of your fears and doubts, my good news to you is that it's never too late to change the course of your life. **If you choose to get over your doubts, and trust that you can, believe me, you can do anything that you set your mind to!**

Importance of Self-Trust

First of all, I want you to realize that there's nothing wrong
with trusting yourself. I understand that we all have the
tendency to second guess ourselves, especially if we've been
committed a lot of mistakes in the past. But keep in mind
that there's no other being in this world that can trust you
more than yourself. Why? Because you're the only one who
can give the right judgement for yourself, you're the only one
who knows your real capability, and you're the only one that
can call the shots on how you want to run your life. In
contrary, you are also the only one who's allowing doubts to
envelope you, therefore limiting you to what you can
become.

So right now, I would really like to encourage you to allow
self-trust to happen in your life. If you want to succeed in
anything, like loving yourself more, improving your
confidence, building relationships, and ultimately, living a
happy life, then the virtue of self-trust is what you want to
have. When you trust yourself, you are giving yourself the
power to control whatever situation you are going to
encounter. You stop playing the victim and you start
choosing whether you want to become miserable or will have
the power to turn a bad situation into something good.

When you practice self-trust you shun away fears and
worries that may cause you to slow down, or worse, trap you
to achieve your goal. Even making decisions becomes easier
for you because you exactly know what you want. You will no
longer second guess yourself because you know that you can
do whatever you set your mind to.

Ways to Practice Self-Trust

You can follow the tips below to regain your trust in yourself again.

- **Self-Reflect**

  Sometimes, the most productive time we have is when we slow down and reflect. One of the ways you can strengthen your self-trust is to find time every day, for example, every morning before you start getting up from bed, to do some reflection. Listen to your intuition. Find peace and dig deep inside for these questions:

  What are you thinking at the moment? Are there any self-defeating thoughts that are cluttering your mind?

  Are these thoughts valid? Or are you just making yourself worry?

  What do you want to do today to feel accomplished? What can you do to make these things happen?

Listen to what you have to answer to these questions.
And when you find them, believe them to be true. Yes,
you can feel accomplished today. Do what you have to
do and put your whole heart into it, because you can!

- ## Be Brave to Take Risks

Yes, you're safe if you don't take risks, but that's it—
nothing will happen in your life if you don't take risks!
But, if you want to make something out of your life,
whether its outcome is good or bad, then you have to
take the leap. And even if taking risks leads you to a
more challenging situation, you'll only be considered
as a failure if you give up. However, if you trust
yourself and pursue whatever you want to accomplish,
even with adversities on hand, then you will surely
emerge as victorious.

- ## Never Be Bounded by Your Mistakes

Again, the only thing that's holding you back to a
better life is yourself. If you allow your past mistakes
bound you, then you're assured that you're not going
to move forward. Be bold, take risks and allow
yourself to make mistakes. Forgive yourself for these
failures, but also learn from them so you will become
wiser the next time around.

- **Take One Step at A Time**

Even if I encourage you to trust yourself and take risks, you are still the best judge of yourself. If you think that you'll be more successful in trusting yourself more when you take one small step at a time, then by all means do it.

If you feel that jumping on a new venture in life is a big goal for you because you don't trust yourself yet, but still you want to do it in the future, then why not go slow and achieve one mini-goal at a time? These mini-goals should help prepare you and move you closer to your ultimate goal.

- **Nurture Yourself**

How can you learn to trust yourself again, if in the first place you don't take care of your own needs? On your journey to self-trust, make sure that you also have a well-balanced life. Allow yourself to have the time to be detached from the stressful world, take care of your body's needs—eat well, drink lots of water, and exercise.

Finally, it's not only your physical needs that you want to take care of. You also want to nurture your emotional and mental needs. Find time to meditate and listen to your inner self, **have the attitude of gratitude** (think of the things, even the simplest ones, that you are thankful for), and recite positive affirmations to lift up your spirit.

When you practice self-trust you shun away fears and worries that may cause you to slow down, or worse, trap you to achieve your goal. Even making decisions becomes easier for you because you exactly know what you want.

You will no longer second guess yourself because you know that you can do whatever you set your mind to.

- **Drive the Negativity Out of Your Mind**

As soon as you decide to trust yourself again, you should make a conscious reminder to yourself that any thoughts that would cause you to doubt yourself should be driven away. Catch yourself when you hear yourself thinking of things like: "Am I capable of doing this?", "Am I ready for this?" or "I don't think I have the skills to achieve that goal." And then replace it with positive thoughts such as "I am capable of doing this because I have prepared for this for so long.", "I will never know if I'm ready for this unless I try," and "I was given this opportunity because people believe that I can do it!"

Do you think you're ready to trust yourself again? Are you ready to shun the negative thoughts that have been defeating you all these years?

Are you ready to hold the reigns and take charge of your life? Move to the next chapter to see how!

Chapter 4: Taking Charge of Your Life

For years, or maybe your whole life, you're used to doing whatever other people ask you to do. You do this probably because: a) you're afraid that people will blame you if you fail because you took things into your own hands, b) you don't believe that you have it in you to decide on your own, or c) you're used to following orders so that people will accept you and you will fit in.

Whatever reasons you may have, I want to ask you these questions: Aren't you tired of listening to other people's commands? Is there a small voice inside you that's screaming out wanting you to make decisions on your own? Do feel that you'll be happier when you take charge of your life?

If your answer is "yes", then this is the perfect time for you to take charge of your life. Like I said in the previous chapter, as soon as you get to know yourself better, and established self-trust, you have the capability to call the shots. **You can**

become the captain of your own ship if you want to.

Yes, there could be bumps along the way and challenges will surely be thrown at you left and right, but guess what? All people go through these difficulties. However, what sets other people apart is how well they maneuver themselves through life's rough roads so they end up to their chosen destination.

More often than not, when we experience failures and difficulties we become disconnected with our own voice and seek other voices to tell us how to get out of the situation. There's nothing wrong with seeking help or advice from others, but it becomes dangerous when we begin to trust the opinions of others more than ours. Even if your gut tells you that you know a better solution than what others tell you, you still opted to listen to their opinions because you don't trust yourself anymore. This becomes a vicious cycle that in the end, you see other people taking charge of your life, instead of you taking the responsibility for your own life.

If you want to hold the reigns of your own life again, feel empowered, and live a fuller life, then follow these suggestions to help you take back the ownership of your life:

- **Build a Strong Connection with Yourself**

  Sometimes, because there are already enough loud voices telling you what to do and how you should decide on things, you often neglect to hear the voice that is most important—**<u>yours.</u>** That's why, if you want to take control of your life again, what you need to do is to build a strong connection with yourself. This may sound funny to you, but this is the only way that you will be able to hear your voice loud and clear even if unsolicited advice from other people will crowd you.

How can you create this strong connection? One of the ways to do this is to have an everyday quiet time. It will only take 10-15 minutes every day and I recommend you do this as soon as you wake up or before you go to bed. Find a place where it's quiet and free from any distractions. You may bring a pen and paper if you want to so that you can write your ideas when they come to you. Use this time to think what you really want in life. How do you want your life to go? Are your decisions aligned to this goal? Are you taking responsibility for your decisions or you are allowing other people to decide for you?

If you repeatedly do this every day, you will eventually have a strong connection with your inner self. You will be able to see a clear roadmap unfold your way because you exactly know which direction you want to go. No failures, challenges, or advice from somebody else can take you away from your goal because you know where you're heading.

• Create a Clear Line Between You and Others

I'm not telling you to avoid relationships just so you can run your life like you want it to. We all need healthy relationships; we need to co-exist with other people. What I'm saying is that, even though you are emotionally attached to other people, it doesn't mean that you're already giving them the authority to take charge of your life. Make sure that you still have what experts call as a "psychic space" where you can still decide on your own, do things the way you want them to, **while still maintaining a healthy and nurturing relationship with other people.**

- **Realize that You Have it in You to Make it Happen**

  Sometimes when we depend too much on other people, we end up disappointed, especially if they don't deliver what we expect them to do. Taking charge of your life means you believe in yourself because you have it in you. Focus on your strengths and abilities, enhance it, and use it to reach whatever you want to achieve.

- **Make Sure that Your Relationships are Healthy**

  Are you friends with people who support you and have a positive effect on you? Or are you surrounded by individuals who often question you and belittle you? If you have relationships like the latter, then this is the time that you slowly cut yourself away from that relationship. You want to be with people who are there to help you grow as an individual, to realize your greatest potential, and are there for you even if you fail as many times as you can. Life is hard as it is, don't make it even harder by surrounding yourself with people who are only dragging you down. Remember that you are the one calling the shots now, so you can take yourself out of these unhealthy relationships if you want to.

Stop blaming other people, your failures, and
your past on how your life turned out to be.
Remember that your life is the result of your
choices. If you choose to remain the victim of
your past, then you will remain that way.

On the other hand, if you choose to take charge
of your life and take responsibility for the results
of your actions and decisions, then you have the
likelier chance to live a happy life.

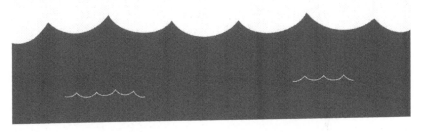

- **Stop Making Excuses and Start Taking
Responsibility**

Of course, **it's easier to say**, "I don't listen to myself
because my judgement isn't always right," **than** "I will
take responsibility for my life and face whatever the
outcome may be." But remember that every time you
make excuses not to take charge of your life, you are
actually allowing yourself to play the victim. You allow
your life to be dictated by other people. Stop blaming
other people, your failures, and your past on how your
life turned out to be. Remember that your life is the
result of your choices. If you choose to remain the
victim of your past, then you will remain that way. On

the other hand, if you choose to take charge of your life and take responsibility for the results of your actions and decisions, then you have the likelier chance to live a happy life.

- **Always Put Your Best Foot Forward**

Finally, if you want to take charge of your life right, put your best foot forward. **Do not allow your fears and worries to keep you from being great.** From now on, whatever you do, just put your heart out and do it. Eventually people will see and appreciate your efforts.

Chapter 5: Embracing Your Uniqueness

How do you define beauty? Is a woman beautiful when she has flawless skin, a perfect body? How do you define a happy life? Is a happy life defined by how much money you have in the bank? How big your house is? Or how many luxury cars you own?

You have to understand that every one of us has different definition of what beauty is and what a happy life is. I don't understand why people try to achieve a certain look or a stature in life to be accepted. Why should you be pressured to be "beautiful" or project a "happy life" when there's not even an absolute definition of those words?

You see, each person is born different. Even twins who look alike are different from each other. They have their own unique personalities, taste, and characteristics. Every individual is born with his or her strengths and weaknesses; so **it's OK to be different!** Of all the billions of people who lived and who are still living on this earth, nobody is born the same. This only means that **you are special!** And it's only up to you if you reject your individuality and be miserable about it your whole life, **or embrace it and celebrate yourself for who you are.**

Why should you accept your uniqueness?

There are a lot of reasons why you should embrace your individuality, some of the reasons are:

- Your individuality is all that you have. When you reject it and fail to appreciate it, you are only lying to yourself.

- Loving yourself for who you are, flaws and shortcomings included, will make you happy. When you learn to appreciate your uniqueness, you will learn to **see way past what you don't have and instead focus on what you were blessed with.**

- Also, when you love yourself, you won't be intimidated or jealous of people who project themselves to have it all. When you begin to accept yourself, you then stop comparing yourself to others because you now understand that each and every one is unique, so there is actually no point in comparing.

- Embracing your individuality will help you learn what you want in life and what role you play in this world.

- Achieving goals also becomes easier when you accept your uniqueness, because you will not waste your time pitying yourself for the things and skills that you don't have, and instead focus on what you have to make things happen.

- Lastly, embracing your uniqueness means you are freeing yourself from trying to win the approval of others because you become content with what you have.

How Can You Embrace Your Uniqueness?

There are actually many ways on how you can embrace your own individuality. The sad thing is, people fail to do these things because they're too occupied trying to "fit in" the definition of what others believe to be as "acceptable". They forget that the only way that others could accept them is when they accept themselves first.

Here are some ways on how you can celebrate your individuality:

- **Find Your Passion**

  Dig deep within you and figure out what you're passionate about. Reflect on your beliefs, your values, and the things you love doing. Don't allow your personal biases or the fear of judgment of others to affect your thoughts. **You will know if you're passionate about a thing when you're willing to do it for the years to come, every single day of your life.**

- **Be True to Yourself**

  Stop making yourself believe that you're happy living a life that you don't actually like, because in the end, you will only make yourself miserable. Stop pretending that you're OK just so you can make other people happy. Find out what will make you happy and pursue it; even if it means getting judged by other people.

- **Stop Comparing Yourself to Others**

  Stop looking at other people and drowning in self-pity because you wish that you have their life. Focus on what you have. **Your strengths, your abilities and talents, these things are what make you special. When you can do this, you'll see the world in a different light.**

- **Reassure Yourself that Being Different is OK**

  When a seed of inferiority comes to you and you begin to question why you're different from the others, always remind yourself that being different is OK. Just imagine a world without individuality, wouldn't that world be so boring? So what if you're unique—we all are! So embrace who you are!

- **Dress the Way You Want To**

  Maybe crop tops and super tight jeans aren't for you,
  then why would you bother wearing them, right?
  Don't allow yourself to blindly follow the fashion
  trends just because everybody thinks it's cool. Dress
  the way you want to. Pick clothes that will speak of
  your personality and will make you feel confident and
  happy when you wear them. **Always keep in mind
  that your smile is still and always your best
  fashion accessory.**

- **Surround Yourself with People that Accept
  You for Who You Are**

  In case you don't know, there are people out there,
  those who care for you and love you, who will accept
  you for who you are. Stop acting like the person that
  you think they will love and just be yourself. True
  friends will accept you even if you allow them to see
  the real you. **Don't waste your tears on people
  who will reject you for being yourself.** You don't
  deserve them in your life.

- **You Can Be Brave and Step Out of Your
  Comfort Zone**

  Lastly, one of the ways for you to totally celebrate your
  uniqueness is to step out of your comfort zone and do
  something you truly desire. Maybe most of your life
  you're just running on routines, going through life on
  auto-pilot that you forget to really do what you want.
  Sometimes in order for you to have a happier life, you
  need to go out of what's practical and follow the

desires of your heart. Stop being of the judgment of others, **believe in yourself and start working on what you want today!**

You see, each person is born different. Even twins who look alike are different from each other. They have their own unique personalities, taste, and characteristics.

Every individual is born with his or her strengths and weaknesses; so it's OK to be different! Of all the billions of people who lived and who are still living on this earth, nobody is born the same. This only means that you are special!

And it's only up to you if you reject your individuality and be miserable about it your whole life, or embrace it and celebrate yourself for who you are.

Chapter 6: Investing on Your Strengths

We all have people we look up to. We admire individuals that have made an impact on the world, or those who started a simple life, but were able to build business empires and became millionaires. Maybe at one point you also envied these people because of how good their life is or how they were able to make a name for themselves. Even though you look up to these people as your inspiration, maybe their life stories also made you feel pity yourself because you didn't have the life they had.

Well, let me tell you this: these people didn't have that kind of life because of fate, these individuals became successful because they chose to be one! You too can make a name for yourself and be an inspiration to many if you choose to invest on your **strengths** and use them to your advantage.

If you start to realize the things that you're good at and begin to use them for your benefit, you will see that achieving goals and becoming successful isn't that hard at all. Don't get me wrong, there will still be a lot of challenges that will come your way before you can say that you've achieved a lot, **but the trip to success will be easier because you have your strengths to hold on to.**

Don't know where you can get a much needed confidence boost? Why don't you try to identify what your strengths and unique abilities are? Knowing your strong points, no matter what they are, will make you less insecure of others and would give you more reason to be proud of yourself.

Are you good at drawing or painting? Do you feel like you have an edge when it comes to analyzing things and problem solving? Or do feel like you're better at explaining things than your colleagues at the office?

Know what your strengths are, develop them further and use them to your advantage.

Investing on your strengths doesn't mean that you're also ignoring your weaknesses. It just means that you're getting the most of what you were given and at the same time, you're also working hard to improve on your flaws.

Benefits of Investing on Your Strengths

Because for years you have denied yourself from self-love maybe you've also forgotten to acknowledge and use the strengths that you were given. For the longest time, maybe you've been doubting yourself if you have any abilities at all. But again, let me remind you that all of us were given **unique gifts,** and it's our choice whether we make something out of this potential or not.

If you're in doubt why you should embrace and invest in your strengths, here are a few reasons why identifying your strengths is important:

- **It Gives You a Confidence Boost**

  Don't know where you can get a much needed confidence boost? Why don't you try to identify what your strengths and unique abilities are? Knowing your strong points, no matter what they are, will make you less insecure of others and would give you more reason to be proud of yourself.

  Are you good at drawing or painting? Do you feel like you have an edge when it comes to analyzing things and problem solving? Or do feel like you're better at explaining things than your colleagues at the office?

  Know what your strengths are, develop them further and use them to your advantage.

- **It Makes You Happy**

  Knowing you're good at something will make you feel

good about yourself. Those self-defeating thoughts that you often entertain will slowly disappear when you begin to focus on your strengths instead of your weaknesses. When this happens, you will surely become a happier person.

- **It Gives You a Clear Direction in Life**

Wonder why some people jump from one career over the other? Or why other people seem to be unhappy to be where they are? That's because they don't know what their strengths are!

For example, when you know that you're good with writing and that you are able to express yourself through words, then maybe you were really made to become a writer or a speaker. Or maybe you're good in the kitchen and even without proper training, you can cook delectable dishes, then most probably you will have a successful career in the restaurant business.

When you can recognize what your strengths are and where are you will work best, then you will have a clear direction in your life as if you have a road map to follow.

- **It Allows You to Grow**

Knowing that you have the skills to make something of yourself will motivate you to push yourself even more. You will look at opportunities that you feared and avoided for so long differently now because you know that you have the assets to make the best of that opportunity. When you start to invest on your strengths, you will surely aim for higher things that you didn't know back then that you can achieve.

- **It Makes Other People Inspired**

When you embrace your strengths and start to make something out of what you have, then you also begin to be an inspiration to others. People will see how you've invested on your abilities to achieve what you set your mind to. Through you, they will see that nothing is impossible if you just believe in yourself.

If you start to realize the things that you're good at and begin to use them for your benefit, you will see that achieving goals and becoming successful isn't that hard at all.

Don't get me wrong, there will still be a lot of challenges that will come your way before you can say that you've achieved a lot, but the trip to success will be easier because you have your strengths to hold on to.

Identifying Your Strengths

Now that you know WHY you should embrace your abilities, the question now is HOW? Here are the steps how:

Step 1: List down your strengths

One of the easiest ways to identify your strengths is to list them down. During your quiet time, get a pen and paper and write down the things that you think you have an edge on. What are your skills that put you above the others? What are your talents or gifts that you think you can use to your advantage? Be real with yourself. Do not underestimate what you can do.

If this activity gives you a sense of accomplishment, then you know it's your strength. If you can achieve a certain task easily or flawlessly, then you can also consider this as your strength. Lastly, if there's a thing that you've been doing all your life and you keep on improving it even without conscious effort, then you can also consider that as your skill.

If you're still having a hard time trying to recognize your strengths, then you can also ask a loved one or a friend to help you identify your strong points.

Step 2: Put your strengths into good use

Now that you have identified which areas you excel at,
it's just about right to put them to your advantage.
You can start nurturing your strengths one at a time.
For example, you've listed down writing as one of your
skills, instead of writing a novel or a self-help book
immediately, you can develop this skill even further
by starting your own blog. Doing this will enable you
to focus and hone your talent even more and would
prepare you for greater things that are ahead of you.

Step 3: Improve on your weaknesses

Like I said, embracing your strengths doesn't mean
ignoring your weaknesses. When you are able to
identify the things that you're good at, you will also be
able to realize what your flaws are. Even though it's
best for you not to focus on these weaknesses, **it
would also be an advantage if you try to
improve on them one step at a time.**

For example, if along the way you realized that one of
your weaknesses is public speaking, but you believe
that earning this skill will help you achieve your goal
of career advancement, then it's just about right to
improve on this weakness. Start practicing in front of
the mirror, practice addressing a speech in front of
your loved ones, or have the courage to speak up and
let others hear what you have to say during meetings.

When you take these little steps, you will see yourself turning this weakness into your strength.

Step 4: Set goals and pursue them

When you finally have embraced your strengths and continue to work on your weaknesses, it's about time for you to set high goals for yourself. When you reach this point, no goal will be impossible for you to achieve because you know that you have it in you to attain whatever you set your mind to.

Just remember to remain focused and use setbacks as your foothold to move upwards. **Give yourself no choice but to achieve your goal**. Forget about what you lack and instead focus on your abilities and just continue to strive to attain your greatest potential.

Chapter 7: 10 Habits to Practice Self-Love

Congratulations! Now that you've finally reached the last chapter of this book, I believe that you already have it in you to love, forgive, and trust yourself again. While there are so many things that you have yet to overcome, deciding to love yourself again is a big leap towards a happier life.

To make things easier for you, I'd like to share with you the 10 habits that you can practice daily to make self-love less of an effort to you, but a part of your everyday life.

1. Take Care of Yourself

This seems to be a no-brainer, but sometimes people often forget to take care of themselves when they are too occupied with other things or when they are wallowed up in self-pity.

Make it a point to find time to take care of yourself. It could be as simple as having a long relaxing bath after a tiring day at work, getting a new haircut for a fresh look, or going shopping for nicer clothes. Just take care of yourself and you'll feel better every day.

Embracing your strengths doesn't mean ignoring your weaknesses. When you are able to identify the things that you're good at, you will also be able to realize what your flaws are. Even though it's best for you not to focus on these weaknesses, it would also be an advantage if you try to improve on them one step at a time.

2. Improve Your Posture

Slouching and keeping your head down can directly affect your confidence. Whenever you find yourself in poor posture, just hold your shoulders back and hold your head up high and you'll surely have an immediate boost in your self-esteem.

3. Exercise

Lots of people exercise to be fit and lose weight, **but did you know that exercising can make you feel good about yourself too?** When you exercise, your brain releases hormones that make you feel happy. Make it a point to at least have a 15-30 minute physical activity every day to feel better about yourself.

4. Give Yourself a Break

Maybe you've enslaved yourself too much. Why don't you take a much-needed vacation? Don't feel bad when you do this because everybody needs to recharge. Take this opportunity to unplug from your stressful life and recollect yourself again. Don't be afraid to spoil yourself because you deserve it!

5. Be Mindful with Your Thoughts

Again, even if negative thoughts only occur in your mind, it doesn't mean that it has no direct effect on your life. Whenever you catch yourself entertaining negative views, stop. Before you believe in them and fall victim to your self-defeating thoughts, try to counter them with questions that will help put your thoughts back into perspective. Ask yourself: "**Are there any evidences that support my worries? Is there any truth in**

what I am thinking right now or am I just too anxious about things?"

Doing this will help you get a more realistic and practical view of things and will control your negativity.

6. Try to Focus on Solutions Instead of the Problem

This is one thing you definitely have to change. One of the ways for you to help improve yourself and also avoid unwanted stress, you have to start focusing on the solutions instead of the problem ahead of you. Don't take challenges as a dead end, use them as a way to make the situation better. **Remember, it's all about perspective.**

7. Have Daily Quiet Time

Like I said earlier, having a quiet time (as short as 20 minutes a day) where you write down your thoughts is one way of creating a strong connection with your inner self. Use this time to build your confidence and defeat the negative self-image that you have for yourself. Listen to your thoughts, identify the things you are passionate about, recognize your strengths and use them to your advantage.

8. Always Be Thankful

An attitude of gratitude can make a big difference in your life. Instead of focusing on what you don't have, why don't you make it a habit of being thankful even in the smallest things that life has blessed you with? Take every chance you can to be grateful. Be grateful for the job you have that pays the bills, be thankful because you have friends that love you and accept you for who you are.

9. Practice Kindness

Whenever you become kind to other people, you also start to be kind to yourself. You don't always have to go big whenever you show kindness. Holding the door for other people, smiling to a stranger and greeting them good morning, or letting your friends know you're there for them are some ways of how you can practice kindness.

10. Choose to Forgive Yourself Every Day

Lastly, it's always good to choose to forgive yourself every day. Keep in mind that we all have the capacity to fall short and make mistakes, so don't be too hard on yourself when you disappoint yourself or someone else. **Mistakes happen for us to realize what is right, they are there to teach us lessons and make us better.**

Don't let your failures control you. Allow yourself to detach from your mistakes and move forward in your life.

An attitude of gratitude can make a big difference in your life. Instead of focusing on what you don't have, why don't you make it a habit of being thankful even in the smallest things that life has blessed you with?

Take every chance you can to be grateful. Be grateful for the job you have that pays the bills, be thankful because you have friends that love you and accept you for who you are.

Conclusion

Thank you again for reading this book! I hope that this book was able to make you realize that the only key to improving your confidence, having great relationships, and entirely living a happier life is through self-love.

Do not play the victim of the unfortunate things that happened to you in the past, you have the choice to overcome these things, correct your mistakes, and move on to a better life. There's nothing you can do to alter the past, but you have the power to make something of yourself today so you can have a great future ahead of you. Never let any seed of doubt hinder you from becoming what you ought to be. **Invest on your strengths, and start taking charge of your life.** Embrace your abilities and your individuality and then you'll see that you can achieve whatever you set your mind to.

You are destined for great things if you believe that you are! Let go of your doubts, start loving yourself today and live a happy life that you deserve!

About the Author

For me, the hardest part of being a mom is learning how to manage my own emotions. I yelled at my son, I felt horrible, guilty and so stressed and tired. I started reading lots of self-help books and I have learned a lot.

I want to share what I have learned throughout the years with my readers; I hope my books can help you deal with your day-to-day challenges, and make you feel happy again, you can create a home full of peace and love for the whole family.

Visit my website here for more self-improvement tips and advice:

http://improve-yourself-today.com

Did you enjoy reading this book? Can I ask you a favour?

Thanks for purchasing and reading this book, I really hope you find it helpful.

If you find this book helpful, **please help others find this book by kindly leaving a review.** I love getting feedback from my customers, loved it or hated it! Just Let me know. and I would really appreciate your thoughts.

Thanks in advance

Jennifer N. Smith

Did you enjoy reading this book?

Please help others find this book by kindly leaving a review.

Thanks in advance

Jennifer N. Smith

If you want to learn more about how to change your life to positive thinking, this book will teach you everything from

CHANGING YOUR LIFE THROUGH POSITIVE THINKING

How To Overcome Negativity and Live Your Life To The Fullest

JENNIFER N. SMITH

how to overcome negativity, how we sabotage our efforts toward positivity by talking negatively to ourselves, how stress and anxiety can affect our lives, and how staying healthy can help us be more positive, to the physical and mental tricks that you can employ to begin utilizing positive thinking in your life today.

Positive thinking can change us physically and emotionally, and they can provide us with a longer life and a plethora of physical health benefits.

If this sounds or something that you would like to read more about, Changing Your Life Through Positive Thinking has the answers you need about how you can empower yourself and leave negativity behind you forever.